Katharina Dobrick

Smiling Words

Float from Heart to Heart

Poems

Katharina Dobrick

Was born in 1947 in Twistringen (near Bremen) and currently resides in Rudersberg/Stuttgart.

Through her confident, loving texts she hopes to encourage her fellow human beings never to lose hope. It would be nice if her positive poems brought you, dear reader, a little joy. It would be a great gift to the author if her poems would make your world a little friendlier.

More information can be found in the internet: http://www.katharinas-buchstaben-welten.de

Bibliographic information from
the Deutsche Nationalbibliothek :
The Deutsche Nationalbibliothek lists
this publication in the
Deutschen Nationalbibliothek;
Detailed bibliographic data can be found
in the internet at http://dnb.d-nb.de.

Imprint:

Copyright© Katharina Dobrick, 2010

Translation: Sarah Fritz

Concept, book design, print layout: Christa Klebor

Production and publisher:

Books on Demand GmbH, Norderstedt

ISBN: 978-3-8391-8098-3

German National Library

My smile

It
Like a good fairy
Is important
For many people
My smile

Moments of Happiness

They
Are the
Dewdrops
Of love
In harmony with our souls

Moments of joy

Arrived

Now
I have
Arrived in verse
And feel great
Joy

Happiness

In my heart

Sounds

A melody

My senses listen,

Feel, perceive

Love, joy, harmony

Souls caress each other in

Happiness

The Moment

In the blink of an eye
In time
Dissolves a breath
Of eternity

My feelings reflected in the
Iris blue of your loving eyes

Love, joy, hope, happiness
Twinkle like stars in the
Moment

Hope

Never abandon your hope

It is solace in the course of life.

It strengthens your will

So you can create new paths.

You can give people peace

Which is the most beautiful thank-you in life.

Then your life has purpose

Since you are a vessel of hope

Life

Endearing
experiences
bring us
closer
together

Tranquility

It is

A balm to me

The injured soul is comforted by

Silence

Dreams DREAMS Dreams Dreams eams

They

Are not

Froth

Rather valuable

Aides to the soul in a rich life

Our dreams

Gratitude

A
Deep feeling
Floods my soul
It smoothes the waves and
The unevenness of life

Traces of My Life

In the
Enchanted garden
Of my own feelings
They lie hidden
Newly discovered

Life traces

Purpose of Life

Help
That you
Yourself can offer
Bestows upon you
Strength and purpose
In your own life

A blissful day

When I awake in the morning cheerful
Laughing my day begins
Able to bring a person joy
That is for me a blissful day

My Soul

My soul
It has wings
Floats therewith
From heart to heart

Swings itself
Across all boundaries
Devotes itself
To people

Brings much joy
To the hearts
Kindles there
A small flame

Peace, warmth and
Much happiness
Is then
Instantly requited.

Neighbourly Love

From

The source

Of our own life joy

It joins people

To one another

In love

Joy of Life

To go through life with positive mean
And all the beautiful things see

Love is thereby our companion guide
Rendering our life more blithe

The joy that we give full of cheer
In our own heart does reappear

Love

Light shines
In
Realization
Remarkable
Experiences

Love

It

Is the

Binding agent in

Relationships

Between people

Love

Love is my magic expression
It is lived, regardless of location

It also exists in all tongues
And, when with laughter it unites

It is the most wonderful team on earth
Stretching to every corner of the universe

It soars out into this world

What great fortune we humans hold

To my great joy there reigns

Peace

Which already exists this day.

My Practiced Neigborly Love

Neighbors
Listen attentively
Encourage and
Emphasize, support
Creative ideas so that
He/she their own
Talents

Recognize and

Search

For solutions

Internal

Self-reflections to

Already be able to

Experience changes

Ray of Hope ope

A
Delicate hint
Full of trust are
Wandering, knowing glances into the

Light

Harmony

Serene

Well-balanced

Peaceful

Moments

Reveal

Apparent

Self

Insight

Inner Peace

Forgiving yourself
Is often difficult.

It is the only way
To find peace of mind

Respect

Risk a journey into the world of
Self realization,
Enjoy the silence in order to
Discover new paths, to follow them,
Be allowed to live them, with newly won
Strength become acquainted with new
people,
To meet and carry on the
Peaceful exchange.

*E*motional Words

My thoughts

Captured in words

Find the way

On a street of stars

Surrounded by beautiful melodies

To the heart

Comforting warmth radiates

Melody of the Heart

On the piano of life

Each heart plays its own melody

Different tact frequencies

Prescribe the rhythm.

When they then find one another

It resounds through the souls

Pleasant and harmonious

A wonderful melody

Still and listen

There plays

The orchestra of hearts

Embrace

Embrace Embrace

In unison with

The hearts

It softly rings

The little bell

Sympathy

All senses are wide awake

Sense and feel

Love, joy and harmony

Souls touch one another.

Warmth of the Heart

A soft heart,
Thus never breaks

There lives in it
Confidence

Relationships

They
Stumbled,
Those relationships
With those most dear
Lonely

Brocken Heart

It is enveloped by iron chains.

Experienced painful memories
Pounded ruts and nails,
Until it despaired in life, the
Broken heart

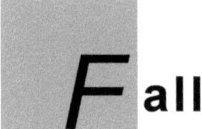**F**all

Strong

Turbulent

Cause creates

Peaceful

Times

Parting

They
Are tired
Caress no more
Now rest forever

Mother's hands

Silenced

Voice of the heart
Silenced
Full to the brim
masked

Will she free herself
From this spell
Will she remain silent
How long?

Will she soon manage
That once again words can sound
Soul waste is removed
Will now follow easier days?

Let us desire for her
That in the concert of the world
This voice will no longer be absent
The mouthpiece of the heart
Never again
Silenced

Image in the Mirror

In the mirror
Of my soul
I look at
YOU
And see
ME

My Little Paradise

In my little paradise
I listen to the birds,
Their songs caress my soul
Here I find my inner peace

I now feel very attached
To the nature that surrounds me
The flowers and their beauty here
Bow down before me
Indulge me with their scents
That now flow through my nose

My Little Paradise

In this splendor it is certainly
The breakfast that I truly enjoy here
The coffee, freshly brewed
With rolls, that taste so delicious
That waken my life spirits

I am very thankful and happy as well
That I am blessed in life
Can experience all of the beauty

With eyes that see well,
With ears that hear others
The nose, it can experience the variety
Of aromas
The mouth that smiles, that senses joy
And shares it in life
The hands allowed to stir, to caress,
Touch, thank for the good experience
The heart, how open it is, to listen,
Feel,
See, to give people hope

My Little Paradise

Found

In the
Commotion of
Daily life
I once again found
Something
Very important
Me

Bridges

Relationships

We can

Reflect upon in peace, not

React chaotically, rather

Act creatively and constructively

Find a new way, to

Live in proximity to people

Dear Neighbors

In my heart arises warmth

When through my little garden I goeth

Side by side with those so dear

The neighbor waves and greets from near.

He cheerfully invites us over

Together we a glass of wine savor.

The moral of this little history

Please my neighbors forget not me.

The Trees of Life

All in a row
They stand
Like pearls
On a string

The trees
That everyone sees

That bear fruit
For we humans only

They are to me
The jewels of
Nature

Course of Life

Colorful

Leaves flutter

Through the air

Fall exhausted to the ground

Know their life has been lived

Find strength in their fellowship

Produce new life

Wishes for the Year

Confidence in every day
Should carry you along the way

Harmony will accompany you
Conflicts will fall away, serenity holds true

Love is a true friend
Makes our life bright again

Health and happiness
Always in mind

Laughter is the medicine in life
Makes hearts free
Is for all of us a blessing

TiME

It gnaws away
In many places
We experience pain
In our time

It makes us forget
The load we carry
Memories it catches
Cushioning our beds
In the fields of transience
In this time

It also heals many wounds
A bandage it often holds ready
So that we can find joy, love
During the course of our time

Help and hold
We do to her
So that we remain
In her favor
Our time

A THANK YOU

From me to
All people
That have until today
Accompanied and supported me.

THANK YOU for your friendship
Love and understanding.
I am so glad that you are here.

A special THANK YOU
To my mentors
Marliese + Erwin, Klari, Gabi Steiner
And the entire team.
THANK YOU for always believing in me.